# HOW TO SURVIVE A
# RUSSIAN FAIRY TALE

## NICHOLAS KOTAR

WAYSTONE
PRESS

## ❦ I ❦

## AT THE WAYSTONE

In a certain kingdom, in a certain land...

You may have heard of Russian fairy tales. At least, you've probably heard of Baba Yaga (even if it's only because of John Wick). Maybe you're intrigued by what you've heard. Maybe you just like fairy tales, especially the ones that you might have not heard yet.

You've come to the right place.

After all, reading fairy tales is almost the same as going on an adventure yourself. And no matter how much you might think that you're above all that, that you left that desire for adventure in childhood, you're wrong. Even Bilbo Baggins, after all, became an accomplished adventurer.

But the realm of Russian fairy tales is perilous. You might think you know who's friend, who's foe. But you'd be wrong. Wolves might be friends. Old grandmothers might be cannibals. And the idiot might be the wisest man in the room.

So let's say you find yourself at the waystone, a boundary between the real world and the world of story. Every road you take from the waystone leads to danger and the potential of great rewards. But you could end up being eaten, chopped into little pieces, or even turned into a goat (hint: avoid forest pools with odd animals grazing next to them). So, the rest of this book is a short guide for your survival. At the end, you'll find the fountain of youth, riches unimaginable, the man or woman of your dreams...and maybe something even more lasting.

But getting there is the real pleasure. Welcome to the weird and wonderful world of Russian fairy tales.

## ❦ 2 ❦

## THE PRE-TALE

You probably know some of the best first lines in literature.

"It was the best of times, it was the worst of times..." (*A Tale of Two Cities*)

"Call me Ishmael..." (*Moby Dick*)

"All happy families are alike; each unhappy family is unhappy in its own way." (*Anna Karenina*)

The arresting beginning is something every writer and story-teller strives to achieve. Russian fairy tales in particular have an unusual way of grabbing the audience's attention. The storyteller begins nearly every story with something called a pre-story. It's not a prologue, though. It's basically a stream of nonsense that has nothing to do with the actual story!

Why do Russians do this, do you ask? Well, Ivan Ilyin, the great Russian philosopher and writer, has a long essay on the spiritual meaning of fairy tales (included in part in the last chapter of this book). In it, he explains that fairy tales in general, and the Russian versions in particular, are far from mere bed-time stories to entertain the kids. They are profound expressions of a nation's mythic consciousness.

To enter into that mythical space, the storyteller breaks all bonds with reality, disorienting the listeners, making them ready to feel the profound meaning of the story, the deeper reality that the plot only hints at.

So, without further ado, here are some of the strangest ways that Russian fairy tales begin.

## THE TEASE AND THE PROMISE

"The story begins from the grey, from the brown, from the chestnut-colored horse. On the sea, on the ocean, on the island of Buyan—there stands a baked bull and a pounded onion. In the side of the bull, there's a sharpened knife. Now, the knife comes out...Would you like to eat?

"This is still not the story, but only the pre-story. If anyone listens to my story, he will receive a sable and a marten coat, a beautiful wife, 100 rubles for his wedding, and fifty more for the party!" (from Afanasiev's *Fairy Tales*)

What on earth does it mean? Well, something like this: get ready for what's coming, and don't dare interrupt. You'll see it all for yourself soon enough!

## THE RHYTHMICAL DANCE

"Granny Alina, where did you go?"

"To the new town."

"What's in the new town?"

"A duck in a skirt, a mallard in a kaftan, a cow in burlap, there's no better cow than she..."

"But this is the pre-story; the story's still to come. Flax tow, flax tow, where do you fly? You sat on a shrub, you sat on a shrub, and you sang like a nightingale.

"Our town, it's not like your town, there the flax tow sings like a nightingale."

*What on earth?*

Well, in other words, it's time to reorder your perception of reality, to go a little bit insane, to get ready for anything, to not be amazed at anything. Then, you'll understand everything...Or not...

## THE INDISCRIMINATELY PUGNACIOUS PRE-STORY

Once upon a time, there lived two peasants. One was Anton, the other—Agafon. "Listen, brother, said Anton. The winds of misfortune blow our way!" And Anton himself shook like a leaf.

"Well, what's the trouble?"

"The hail's coming, and all our wheat's gonna die!"

"What hail? It's just a rainstorm."

"No, hail!"

"No, rain!"

"I don't want to talk to a moron," said Anton, and punched his brother in the face. Neither hail, nor rain came, but the blood poured from their noses and ears.

But this is not the tale, this is only the pre-story. The story is yet to come...tomorrow, after lunch, when you've eaten some soft bread...

So... in this case, what it means is: here, watch. I'm going to mix up all the cards, to throw you into the middle of a stupid argument. After this, you'll be much more willing to believe the incredible events of my story.

## THE INSINUATING INTRODUCTION

In that distant time when the world of God was filled with *leshye*, witches, and mermaids, when the rivers flowed with milk along berry-juice shores, and fried quails flew in the fields—in that time lived a king, his name was Pea, with his queen Anastasya the Beautiful...

This sort of pre-story takes the soul of the listener by the hand, like a child, and leads it to an ancient and wondrous world, almost by magical insinuation or chanting.

That's what fairy tales are like. They lead us in, freeing our imagination to take flight, feeding our souls to their fill. Then, the story leads us back, often finishing in the traditional image of a drunken feast:

*And there I was, and I drank the mead and the beer. But it all flowed down my mustache, and not into my mouth!*

That means that the story is over, and it's time to get sober from our momentary story-drunkenness. After all, we were not really drunk. All the liquor missed our mouths completely...

## ❊ 3 ❊

# A PHRASEBOOK FOR THE WORLD OF FAIRY TALES

So... you've made it past the crazy pre-story. But you still might be a bit confused as you enter the perilous realm of Russian fairy tales.

Russian epic poetry has a specific language that even some Russians find difficult to understand. It gives the stories part of its epic feel, while also grounding it in a very earthy reality, even if that reality is sometimes hard to decipher.

To help you out, here's a cheat sheet. Just in case you ever find yourself lost in the world of Russian fairy tales.

❦

IMPORTANT PHRASES FOR TRAVELERS IN RUSSIAN FAIRY TALES

❦

"I'M VERY ANGRY!" : **"I'M GOING TO CHOP IT DOWN TO A stub!"**

❦

"What a gentleman!" : **"Your bow is well-studied, your cross is straight from the book!"**

❦

"A dangerous woman" : **"A wolf's meal"**

❦

"He's in shock" : **"He shakes his golden curls; he clicks his bejeweled fingers"**

❦

"I'm beside myself" : **"My warrior's heart is boiling!"**

❦

"Bad dog! (or any animal)" : **"You bag of grass!"**

❦

"Would you like to play a game?" : **"Should we not play checkers-chess, those tablets of gold?"**

❦

"Who is that person?" : **"What sort of stink comes from behind my stove?"**

❦

"Hi!" : **"Hail, you brave young warriors!"**

❧

"He opened the door" : **"The door swung around his ankle"**

❧

"Sorry I'm late!" : **"I traveled a straight road, but how that road has lingered!"**

❧

"He's upset" : **"That became for him a great sorrow; it seemed a horrible grief!"**

❧

"She's a ditz" : **"A woman's concerns are dazzling, dazzling, and mercurial"**

❧

Come to think of it, I'm not sure how much of this is useful. But I'm definitely going to start greeting everyone as "brave young warriors." And I think I've found my favorite new insult, you bag of grass!

# ❧ 4 ❧

## BABA YAGA

S o you've survived the pre-story, and you even have a (dubious) phrasebook for unexpected encounters in the dark forest. It's time to meet some of the denizens of that forest.

In the slumbering wood, in the deepest darkness, a hut stands on two chicken feet. In the hut, on the stove, Baba Yaga reclines on the ninth brick. Her legs are bony, her nose has grown all the way up to the ceiling, and she's sharpening her own teeth. She looks like an old woman, but there's something odd about her. Who is she? Is she even an old woman at all?

Baba Yaga is an ambivalent character, and that makes her very interesting. She's definitely scary—her face covered in warts, her crooked nose. She has hands like hooks, a hump on her back. Still, you can't exactly call her a villain. Yes, she constantly threatens to eat Ivan the Prince, or Mashenka, or Vasilissa the Beautiful, but we never actually see her eat anyone. Really, her purpose in the stories is to be a magical helper to the hero, even if her help is not always what's expected.

In Russian fairy tales, the hero first encounters and speaks to forest beasts (hedgehog, rabbit, bear, pike, etc.). Only then can he find the hut standing on chicken feet. After he meets Baba

Yaga, he always has to face some kind of test before encountering the real villains of the stories—Koshchei the Deathless, Zmei Gorynich (the dragon), Likho of the One Eye (evil fate), Kikimora, Leshy (a forest demon). These and other demonic creatures don't belong to the real world. They represent the world of the dead in the fairy tales. Baba Yaga belongs to that magic world, but only partly. One of her legs is bony, the other, fat.

## THE BORDER GUARD OF THE DEAD-LANDS

Baba Yaga is the customs officer of the land of the dead. Her hut is a kind of passport control. In that hut, the hero goes through all the necessary rites to begin his journey into the supernatural world. He washes in the sauna, which symbolizes the washing of a dead body before burial. He eats and drinks in excess, which is a hint at the traditional feast (*pominki*) held after a funeral. He always sleeps inside the strange hut, because night is the witching hour, the time of passage from one state to another. And sleep is a kind of small death.

To acquire superhuman strength, the hero must pass into the world of the unreal, where he will be tested. After all, his own strength is not enough to overcome the obstacles that life has thrown in his path.

## THE ANCIENT WILD MOTHER

Dr. Clarissa Pinkola Estés, a Jungian psychoanalyst and philosopher, has an interesting theory about the origins of Baba Yaga. In her book *Women Who Run With the Wolves*, she writes that Baba Yaga is a kind of prototype of primal womanhood, a being of enormous wild power. "Baba Yaga," she writes, "is the very essence of an instinctive and complete soul. She knows everything that was before. She is a keeper of heavenly and earthly secrets. She inspires fear because she simultaneously personifies a destructive power and the power of creation and life."

Interestingly, it's only the male hero who has to overcome a test in Baba Yaga's house to prepare himself for the encounter with the unreal world. Heroines don't. All they have to do is perform some menial chores, and they automatically receive power and wisdom from their "wild mother."

However, not all heroines survive the encounter. Neither do heroes. Some, without learning the valuable lessons they hear from Baba Yaga, get chopped up into little pieces by their own brothers!

## GODDESS OF WAR?

According to some scholars, Baba Yaga could even have been a goddess of war. Some believe she may have actually been part of the Russian pantheon, having as much power as Perun, the Russian Thor. She may have had her own places of worship. In some myths, she is described as a mistress of the beasts and birds, the hostess of the world of the dead. Sometimes she's a thief of life, but sometimes a giver of life, a helper of heroes.

It's this unpredictability that makes her so fascinating. No wonder so many novelists keep resurrecting her in new and unexpected ways.

## RECENT VERSIONS

In Naomi Novik's recent novel *Uprooted*, Baba Yaga only appears as an idea, an ancestor of the magic that the heroine masters. Still, her mischievous wildness is palpable, making her a character in the story, even if she never actually appears.

One of the more unsettling versions of Baba Yaga in recent literature is in Catherynne Valente's *Deathless*. In it, she's a foul-mouthed Stalinist secret policewoman who regularly jumps on the shoulders of the heroine, pushing her down painfully, like the demons in some of Gogol's short stories.

Not the most pleasant of versions, certainly.

In my own first novel, *The Song of the Sirin*, the Hag is an unequivocally evil version of Baba Yaga. At least one reader chided me for making her so one-sided. I think she's right, too. So I had her come back in a more comical role in *The Heart of the World*, my third novel. It's one of my favorite scenes in the book, a respite of humor in an otherwise dark middle chapter of my series.

## 5

# SEVEN OBSTACLES FOR THE HERO OF A RUSSIAN FAIRY TALES

So you've made it to Baba Yaga's hut on chicken feet. Instead of eating you, she's given you a magic horse or a magic handkerchief or a magic comb. But now the really hard work begins. Wouldn't it be great to have some sort of a map for your adventures?

Well, here's the next best thing.

Turns out there are only a small number of obstacles that you'll have to overcome. Not that they're easy, mind you.

The fairy tale begins with a picture of universal prosperity, a static image of perfection. But every fairy tale hero must always face a terrible calamity. From this moment, the story begins its forward momentum. The hero goes on his journey, where he will have unusual encounters, hindrances, and trials. These obstacles, and the magical means that he uses to overcome them, are the essence of the Russian fairy tale, giving it a richness and a unique flavor.

## THE FOREST

After leaving his home, the hero of the story, whether he is Ivan the Prince or the girl kicked out by her evil stepmother, goes "wherever their eyes can see." She or he always ends up in the dark, dangerous forest. The forest is an enemy of men, an unknown power, a hidden threat. The forest is an obstacle for the hero on his way to the mythical "thrice – ninth kingdom," the kingdom of the dead.

Therefore, the forest is impenetrable, and the hero can only get through with magical help. The only positive thing about the forest is that it's also an effective way of losing enemies. So, we have the famous fairy tale trope of Ivan the Prince throwing a magical comb behind him, and that comb becoming an impenetrable forest. Problem solved!

## THE OPEN FIELD

In some stories, the first hindrance is not a forest, but an open field. In this open field stands a waystone with an inscription: "Whoever goes straight will be cold and hungry. Whoever goes to the right will remain alive, but his horse will die. Whoever goes to the left will die, but his horse will remain alive."

The hero is at the parting of the ways. He must choose the correct path. In fact, the open field is itself an obstacle. It is an unknown foreign space, open and vulnerable to attack from mystical powers. It is here that the hero will always die on his way home. His enemies (often his jealous brothers) will kill him and chop him into little pieces. However, this death is often a precursor to his resurrection by Living Water, but only if he shared his bounty with others along the way and made sure to make friends with the magical denizens of the forest, the talking animals.

## THE OCEAN, THE OPEN SEA, OR A RIVER OF FIRE

On his journey, the hero may find a river-spirit, a river of fire, or even a river of milk, beer, honey, or wine. Finally, he might even find the ocean. These are all symbols of chaos. However, the hero overcomes even these obstacles thanks to the magical help he acquires on the way.

Part of the reason for this is that the hero's journey is a symbol of man's mastery over nature. In one story, a wise woman gives the hero a skein of wool that rolls by itself, all the way into the water. After it enters the water, the waters part, and even Ivan the Idiot can pass through unharmed.

## THE INSURMOUNTABLE MOUNTAIN

Dimitri the Prince rides and rides, and suddenly he sees before him a mountain so large that his eye cannot see the summit. Of course, this is not a mountain you can simply ride around. After all, this mountain is the center of the universe, the axis of the world. It is an image of creation in its entirety.

The mountain has three parts. The top of the mountain is the residence of the divine, the bottom of the mountain is the world of the dead, the center is the world of the living. Only he who has received the blessing of the Heights can dare to begin scaling this mountain.

Whenever someone gives our hero a command: "Go there, I know not where, bring that, I know not what," it means he must seek this mountain, which is nothing other than the entrance into the underground kingdom, the kingdom of death.

The insurmountable mountain theme is central to my third novel, *The Heart of the World*.

## THE WALL THAT CANNOT BE CLIMBED OVER

Whether the hero has to acquire magic apples or Living Water or whether he has to enter into the tower of the beautiful Princess, he has to first scale a wall that cannot be climbed over. In the tales of Ivan the Idiot, the hero always has an unfair advantage: his horse can jump higher than the wall. This is more than simply a convenient exit from a difficult situation. By jumping over this wall, the hero demonstrates his prowess, his worthiness to win the bride by any means necessary.

## THE FLOWERING GARDEN

Behind this insurmountable wall, the hero often finds a garden. Even though the garden is a cultivated place, not the wilderness, it still plays the role of an obstacle for the hero. In many different fairy tales, the garden is the domain of the princess whom the hero has to win.

He can reach her unreachable tower in different ways. Either he flies in on a falcon, or he transforms into a falcon, or he rides a horse with four wings. Sometimes he doesn't even have to do that. In the tale *Ivan the Prince and Elena the Beautiful*, the gray wolf does all the hard work. He carries her from her magical garden to the waiting prince.

However it happens, he always marries the princess in the end. Even though the garden is the proper domain of the princess, it is a hindrance for the hero, a foreign place. But after marriage, it becomes their shared space.

## ❧ 6 ❧

# THE MYTHOLOGY OF WATER

I did say that there were only a few obstacles on your way as a hero in a Russian fairy tale. But it's worth talking about one of them a little more. Water.

Water is perhaps the most mythologized element in Russian legends. In my own first novel, *The Song of the Sirin,* Living Water plays a pivotal role. It does in the other books as well. But there is also something called the Water of Death, which plays an important role in nearly all the tales. In any case, it's not surprising that for the ancient Slavs, water loomed large in their stories and legends.

## THE SOURCE OF ALL THAT IS

First of all, water is the source of all that exists. As such, it is tied up in all manner of creation legends. According to the Slavs, it corresponds to primordial chaos, the beginning of the world. In this sense, the ocean is clearly opposed to the organized space of land. Interestingly, since most of Russia is landlocked, there is no separate idea for "ocean" and "sea." In fact, a legendary region called "Ocean-sea" is the bedrock of the world. On it, the earth is established on the backs of three (or seven) whales.

In the *Stone Book*, a book of ancient spiritual poetry collected in the 17-18th centuries, we read the following quote:

"Ocean-sea is the mother of all seas. The sea has covered the whole wide world, that sea reached out to all lands."

What's missing in English is that "Ocean-sea" is feminine and is often compared to a mother (like Earth itself, for that matter).

As for the mythological origin of this Ocean-sea, it comes from somewhere very far away. Still, the sea is not the end of the world, because there are magical lands (possibly Eden) beyond that primordial sea. Another legend has the origin of the sea in the far North, probably in the same place where Koschei the Deathless, the ultimate villain in Russian tales, built his palace on top of crystal mountains. This version is probably not so ancient, dating to a time when the Rus had reached the Arctic circle in their wanderings.

## THE CASPIAN SEA

The Caspian Sea holds a special place in the mythological imagination of ancient Slavs. The sun rises from the Caspian sea. Under this sea is a copper house in which the Serpent of Fire has been chained, while under this Serpent is hidden a seven-ton key to the palace of Prince Vladimir, as well as the armor of the *bogatyrs* (epic warrior heroes) of Novgorod. If one can catch a swan and force it to fly to the Caspian Sea, it will attack the Serpent of Fire and get the key for you. Whoever claims the *bogatyr's* armor will be essentially unbeatable in war.

Interestingly, in some version of this tale, it's not a Swan, but a Raven who must go into the depths. For those of you who have read *The Song of the Sirin* and the rest of the series, this should be a fascinating bit of lore. After all, both the Raven and the Swan as archetypes play important roles in the fate of the world.

There is yet another bird associated with the Caspian Sea— the Eagle. The Eagle was formed from the waves. After its birth, it threw a lightning bolt into the wet earth, which caused a fire that gathered into storm clouds, from which came the rain that gives life to the entire world.

## THE ISLAND OF BUYAN

The Ocean-sea is especially known for the Island of Buyan, which stands at its center. This island is the source of nature's essence, containing the mythical incarnations of the spring storms, thunder, and the winds. The mother of all birds, Gagana, who has a metal beak and copper talons, finds her home there. The eldest of all Ravens also lives there, making sure the Serpent of Fire stays chained in the depth of the Ocean-sea.

Buyan is a magical island, and not surprisingly in pagan Rus, it was often invoked in prayer. It also often appears as an image in fairy tales and epic poetry.

## WATER AS BOUNDARY

Water is also a boundary between worlds. The space between heaven and earth is bordered by water, as is the space between life and death. Water also divides the epochs in a person's life. Ritual washing was a necessary part of coming into the world, entering the marriage state, and being buried. Overcoming water in some form is one of the most common heroic motifs in Russian fairy tales.

Water from the heavens was considered to be life-giving, as

opposed to water on or under the earth itself. Rain is the mythical image of the union between the heavens and the earth, a masculine image of sowing. In fact, the drops of rain are traditionally no different from seeds that give rise to grains necessary for life.

The first rain of the day, in fact, was considered to have powerful energy. It could make your face younger and more beautiful and give health to the body. It could even grant good fortune to one's fate. This is why people always hurried to be outside for the first rain. It's also probably why, to this day, "magic water" still persists in people's imaginations.

In fact, I was surprised and amused to hear from a person otherwise well educated in the order of church services that on the day of Christ's Baptism, you had to take a shower at midnight on the night before the feast to get the full amount of divine grace. Of course, that has absolutely nothing to do with Church tradition, but it's fascinating to see how the ancient fascination with water persists through the ages. To this day, any time water is blessed in churches, you can expect a lot of people to be in attendance.

## "MAGIC WATER"

In pagan Rus, ritual washing was considered necessary on the second day of every spring and summer solstice. Later, it was still considered important to bathe on the day of Ivan Kupala, the day before the beginning of the Saints Peter and Paul fast, and on the mid-point of the period between Easter and Pentecost.

Pagan priests used to counsel people to bathe in rivers and lakes during the rain, as well as to wash from a silver basin before every new moon. It was supposed to be an excellent remedy for bad skin. (It reminds me of the scene in *The Dawn Treader* where

Lucy reads the book of the sorcerer and is tempted by a vision of herself as a great beauty, like Susan).

Of course, these sorcerer-priests were also notoriously unreliable when it came to "water divination." The expression "to beat water with a mortar in a pestle" (which is found in other cultures as well with slight variations) referred to a pagan practice of "preparing magic water" by beating it. It was often found to be lacking in any magic whatsoever, so the expression came to mean "engaging in a pointless act" or "wasting one's time."

## WATER AS A SOURCE OF POWER

So here's where you, as a traveler through the tales, can get some real practical knowledge.

Some "waters" are especially important. "March water" is supposed to protect people from all the diseases that were locked in the snowy hills during winter. Water melted from snow is thus a kind of vaccine, covering people against the winter ills.

Water is also considered important in determining man's fate. This water, called "the water of contention," is taken from the confluence of two rivers. This kind of water is especially useful in telling a person on his death bed whether or not he will get better or die.

Dew was usually considered as potent as the earth itself in giving superhuman strength. Young women used to gather it by dragging a piece of cloth over morning grass, then they'd wring it out into a cup and give it to the sick to drink. However, some dew was dangerous to drink. It was called "Iron Water," and it only appeared on the mornings between May 23 and 25th (for some reason). Children especially would fall sick from such water, as well as domestic animals and trees. Only a pagan priest could heal from such diseases.

## LIVING AND DEAD WATER

All the many supernal qualities of water are concentrated in the folk image of "Living and Dead Water." These two versions of water are sometimes also called "Living and Whole Water," since Dead Water first makes a person whole, then brings him back to life. The reference here is to the extremely common fairy tale trope of the hero being chopped into pieces by his enemies (or his brothers) to prevent any sort of supernatural help from coming to him.

So what you need, if you've gotten chopped up, is to have someone pour Dead Water on you. That'll make all the pieces grown back together. Then Living Water will bring you back to life.

Living Water water is similar in its qualities to ancient Greek ambrosia or nectar. It gives great physical strength, heals wounds, and returns life to the dead. According to the fairy tales, Living Water is brought by Thunder, Hail, and Wind (in their personified, fairy-tale incarnations). Alternately, their "symbolic animals" would bring it—the falcon, the eagle, or the raven (so, like I said, make sure to get nice and friendly with them. If you have three sisters, see if you can marry them off to the birds).

## THE UNDERWATER KINGDOMS

It's not surprising, given water's extensive power both to heal and to destroy, that it should eventually get its own kingdom in the mythological consciousness of Russia. One of the earliest animal symbols of this world is the lizard (or serpent). He is the lord of the waters and all the inhabitants of all waters. There was even a cult of the serpent in Novgorod as late as the 13th century.

In ancient times, the serpent was a symbol of the chaos at the beginning of the world. (He swallows the sun and only returns it in the morning). But in the Novgorodian version, he became an actual "King of the Waters." The king and the serpent-lizard eventually became two separate characters.

He was the lord of all seas, rivers, lakes, and head of all their inhabitants. His crystal palace was found in the depths of the sea. These depths are illuminated brighter than the sun by gems that shine with their own light. His main job is to increase his kingdom by forming new lakes and rivers. He is married, but has no children.

His Queen of the Waters has her own, and very interesting, mythological existence. Sometimes, she even rules alone, without any king. Under the headboard of her bed lies the source of Living Water. Sometimes, it even flows directly from her hands and feet. The way to her underwater palace is nearly always guarded by a twelve-headed dragon. (Perhaps there's a silent wink here to the fate of her husband). Interestingly, despite his being underwater, he still breathes fire.

This connection between the purifying and destructive forces of fire and water is present in nearly all the tales.

Now that you're all caught up on the importance of water, you'll need to learn about some of the creatures that inhabit water. As you might expect, most of them are carnivorous and will do everything in their power to stop your adventure even before it begins.

## MERMAIDS

The name "*rusalka*" (mermaid) appeared in Russian mythology pretty late, probably from the West. From the beginning, they were believed to be the souls of drowned young women. Most of the time, Russian mermaids were represented as physically beautiful, with long, greenish hair. Some of them had fish-like characteristics as well.

They can transform (shape-shifting is a common feature of dark powers) into squirrels, fish, rats, frogs, and birds. If they meet a man, they may sometimes be inclined to tickle him. But before they tickle him (sometimes to death), they often put him through a kind of ordeal. Sometimes the ordeal involves guessing riddles.

Not all mermaids are beautiful, however. In some West Slavic traditions, there is a fantastically ugly version of a mermaid. She is old, hump-backed, cross-eyed, dirty, dressed in rags. In some versions, she has metal breasts, in others, her old withered breasts are so long she has to throw them over her shoulder. She is definitely the most dangerous kind of mermaid. She's the sort of creature you frighten children with at night.

WATER SPIRITS

These are called "*Shilikuny*," and they share both earthy and watery characteristics. These are spirits of a definite demonic character. Interestingly (this is a point that keeps showing up in Russian mythology), they are associated with both water and fire. Short in stature, their primary place of residence is in cracks in the ice of rivers and lakes. They are said to have cone-shaped heads and horses' hooves, and they often breathe fire.

They are also not limited to water, like most mermaids. Travelers could encounter them on crossroads and in the depths of the forest.

Oddly enough, in some areas of Russia, these spirits used to be considered good spirits. Some young women left their spinning wheels outside at night, hoping to get all their yarn spun by the Shilikuna by the morning.

## VILA

These are similar in some ways to mermaids. The vila exist in the mythologies of nearly all Slavic groups, not just Russians. They are especially beautiful, and they live in water and in forests near the water. They're a kind of water nymph with some bird-like qualities. Their bodies, which look very young, are dressed in white robes that are almost transparent. They can flash like lightning and have long hair unbraided over their back and chest.

More frighteningly, they often have either horse hooves or goat-hooves (indicative of their evil nature). But they try to hide them with their flowing white clothes. Vila are supposed to be born of a union of dew with grass (interesting, considering dew was also considered a form of magical water).

They also have beautiful voices and their song is a kind of Siren song. If a man is seduced by them, he loses all joy in life and eventually dies. However, if the vila find a man interesting, they can be extremely useful. They teach all kinds of practical knowledge.

## AND... PHARAOHS?

This is the strangest of the lot. After Christianity had taken root, a new and very odd form of water spirit appeared in the popular imagination. These are called Pharaohs. They have nothing to do with Egypt, other than the fact that they probably appeared after Russians first heard the biblical telling of the Israelites crossing the Red Sea.

Basically, someone probably asked the question: what happened to the Pharaoh's armies who were drowned in the Red Sea? For lack of a better (or more imaginative) answer, folk imagination took over. They became half-human, half-fish creatures that could also appear on land in the forms of cats and bears. They were, naturally enough, nearly always dangerous.

# SEVEN SUPERHERO WARRIORS
# OF RUSSIAN FAIRY TALES

Y ou've got your map, your phrasebook, and you know just how dangerous water can be. Good. You're well on your way.

But it might help if you knew about some of the other heroes who ventured into the sleeping forests before you. At least you can start getting an idea of what sort of hero makes it to the end of the stories without being eaten.

Let's start with the *bogatyrs*, the extremely strong warriors of epic Russian folk poetry.

## SVIATOGOR—THE GIANT WARRIOR

A terrifying giant, Sviatogor is as large as a mountain. In most of the tales, he has grown so huge that the earth can no longer hold him, and he lies half-buried, waiting for death. There are reasons to believe that Sviatogor is a Russian version of the Biblical Sampson, although it's difficult to determine exactly what his origins are. His most important purpose in the stories is to pass on the ancient power of the gods to the new warriors that come with the Christianization of Rus.

## MIKULA SELIANINOVICH

Mikula appears in two stories, one with Sviatogor, and another with Volga Sviatoslavich. He's remarkable not so much for his strength as for his limitless endurance. He is the first peasant bogatyr, a great warrior-ploughman. His great endurance, together with Sviatogor's titanic strength, indicate that their story probably came from old myths about the god of the earth and the patron-god of farmers. But if Sviatogor is a representative of the old, "mythic" world of the gods, Mikula is very human. He's a kind of personification of the beauty of the farming lifestyle, into which he pours his considerable strength.

The fact that he is a warrior only secondarily is something I find interesting. There are elements of this sort of warrior in the character of Tarin in my first novel, *The Song of the Sirin*.

## ILYA MUROMETS

Ilya Muromets is the most important protector of the Russian land against enemies (most of whom were nomadic Asian tribes that harassed Rus for centuries). Although he is definitely a historical character, his story is still steeped in myth.

As the tale goes, he sat paralyzed for thirty years, then received his power from Sviatogor directly. In addition to his physical strength, he has remarkably strong morals. He is calm, firm, simple, non-acquisitive, fatherly, restrained, generous, independent. Even so, he has a temper that sometimes gets the better of him.

In one famous story, he gets angry at Prince Vladimir and retaliates by knocking the crosses off of St. Sophia Cathedral with an arrow. In the cycle of his stories, his character's piety begins to take center stage later. Perhaps he was trying to atone for the sin of defacing the church? The historical Ilya did, eventually, become canonized by the Orthodox Church as a monk-saint.

## DOBRYNIA NIKITICH

He is a *bogatyr* with a gentle heart. Even his name hints at his gentleness (*dobry* means "kind") . Though he has great physical strength, he "will never insult a fly," he is "the protector of the widows and the orphans, and of all damsels in distress." Dobrynia is also an artist—he has a beautiful singing voice and plays the *gusli* (Russian harp). He is one of the only noble-born *bogatyrs*, a model of the prince who is also master of the *druzhina* (warrior band).

He has a fascinating relationship with his wife, who was herself a warrior. But that story's for a different chapter.

## ALYOSHA POPOVICH

Alyosha is often connected in the popular imagination with Ilya Muromets and Dobrynia Nikitich. He is the youngest of the *bogatyrs*. Therefore, he's not quite as much a superman as the rest of them. He is cunning, egotistical, and likes to make money for himself.

On the one hand, he is remarkably bold and courageous. On the other, he is proud, meddlesome, and even a bit crude. He likes to provoke people and is easily angered. Ultimately, he becomes a slave of his shortcomings. In particular, if Dobrynia is a protector of women, Alyosha tends to take advantage of them, though he is never a particularly successful lover.

Of all the *bogatyrs*, he ends up the most pitiful.

⊗⊗⊗

## MIKHAILO POTYK

One of the lesser known warriors, he is best known for killing dragons. Of all the *bogatyrs*, he is perhaps the only one that seems to be a transplant from hagiographic literature (there was a Bulgarian saint, Michael from Potuka, who was one of many warrior-saints to have battled a serpent and won). The difference between him and Ilya Muromets is that no one pretends that Mikhail Potyk was a real historical character.

He is a restless man, a wanderer, and a pilgrim. It's possible that his name was originally "potok," which in the old Russian means "landless" or "nomadic." In some ways he is an idealized pilgrim, an image that holds an important place in the Russian imagination. There is also a version of the tale written by Alexei Tolstoi that imagines Mikhailo as a time-traveling warrior.

⊗⊗⊗

## CHURILA PLENKOVICH

Other than the "elder" and "younger" *bogatyrs*, there's another category of supermen that were "out-of-towners" or mercenaries. Churila is one of these. Their names always indicate the place they come from. In the case of Plenkovich, he comes from Surozh, on the Crimean Peninsula. Unlike nearly all other *bogatyrs*, Churila is a fop, an old Russian Don Juan. The tales describe him as having "skin like snow, eyes like a falcon's, eyebrows black as sable." To keep his complexion pleasingly pale, he actually has a servant following him around with a parasol, to protect him against the sun.

The famous Russian critic Vissarion Belinski noted that Churilo was the most "humane" of all the *bogatyrs*, especially with respect to women. It seems he dedicated his life to them. He never utters a single crude word or expression. On the contrary, he acts in some ways like the traditional knight of the Western troubadour tradition.

Women-storytellers used to prefer his tales to nearly all others.

BEFORE WE GO FURTHER INTO THIS GUIDE ON HOW TO SURVIVE an adventure set in a Russian fairy tale, here's a short historical detour about the three most famous *bogatyrs* of the seven already mentioned.

## ALYOSHA POPOVICH

There are two major labors for which Alyosha is famous—the defeat of Tugarin Zmei (a particularly fierce dragon) and the abominable Idolishche (literally, "Great Idol"). These are mythologized versions of actual historical events that occurred around the tenth century.

According to *The Chronicle of Past Times*, a son of a nobleman in Prince Vladimir Monomakh's court named Olberg Ratiborovich killed the Polovetsian Khan Itlar during peace talks by shooting at him through a hole in the roof. The name Itlar, when hyperbolized to show how terrible he is, becomes "Itlarishche the Abominable" which is very close to "Idolishche" (Great Idol). This historical event probably became the tale of Alyosha Popovich and the Great Idol. It fits also because Alyosha kills his enemy within the walls of a palace, not on the field of battle.

This is the only time an enemy is not killed in battle in the epic poems.

Alyosha's second great labor is the defeat of Tugarin Zmei. The prototype of this dragon-like enemy is also a Polovetsian Khan, named Tugorkhan, from the dynasty of the Sharukhans (a name that means "serpent" or "dragon" in Polovetsian). So it all fits. Olberg (a pagan name) was softened to the Christian "Olesha," becoming, eventually, Alyosha.

## DOBRYNIA NIKITICH

The historical chronicles do mention a Dobrynia, an uncle of Prince Vladimir. This historical Dobrynia had a different patronymic, not Nikitich, but "Malkovich". The Malkovichi hailed from the village of Nizkinichi, which was probably transformed by the oral storytellers into "Nikitich".

The historical Dobrynia played an important role in the history of old Rus. According to *The Chronicle of Past Times*, it was he who encouraged Novgorod (a very independent-minded city) to accept the lordship of Grand Prince Vladimir. He may have orchestrated the political marriage of Vladimir to the Polovetsian princess Rogneda. He was also instrumental in the baptism of Novgorod.

## ILYA MUROMETS

*How is a Bogatyr also a Saint?* The word *bogatyr* immediately calls to mind superhuman strength and boldness, but etymologically, it may have something in common with the Russian word *Bog* (God) and *bogaty* (rich). That is, it could etymologically mean "a man who is rich in God." The Russian folk, historically speaking, pick up words carefully, and often the deeper meaning of words becomes slowly obvious over the course of centuries. The word *bogatyr* appeared in the Chronicles in the 13th century and came to mean "a person gifted with great riches and a divine abundance of physical strength." It is said that the *bogatyr's* strength is not merely physical. He only defeats his enemies because he stands on the side of the truth. And, as the Russian saying goes, "God is not in strength, but in truth."

*Why did Ilya Muromets sit on a stove for thirty years?* The traditional Russian stove has a seating ledge that is the warmest place in the often cold Russian hut. It is also the place where the loafers and drones of fairy tales spend their existence (more on them later). Why did such a folk hero as Ilya Muromets sit on a stove for thirty years? According to the tale, he could not walk for his first thirty years.

Interestingly, recently scientists examined the relics of St. Ilya of the Kiev Caves and noticed pronounced curvature in his lower back and some very obvious bone spurs on the vertebrae. This could mean that in his youth, the saint was effectively paralyzed. The wanderers who came to heal Ilya in the folk tale could have been, according to one version, folk healers who basically performed an adjustment on his backbone and helped him to learn how to walk again. The more traditional version is that he was healed by a miracle.

Another odd nickname that Ilya Muromets has gathered in the tales is Ilya Chobotok, which means "the boot." He received this nickname after he was surprised by some enemies before he had a chance to dress in the morning. He managed to put on one boot, but not the other, and having no other weapon at hand, he beat all of them off with the second boot. We even find this story in a document in the Kiev Caves Monastery. In the tales, this is not the only offhand object he uses to beat back his enemies. One of the epic poems has him defeat a band of thieves with his helmet alone.

Not everyone associates this legendary folk figure with St. Ilya of the Orthodox Church. This division between the legend and the man happened in large part because the Soviet authorities spared no effort to convert the saint into a mythical figure. And so, he needed to be secularized, de-Christianized. For example, a central event in his cycle of tales is his miraculous healing from paralysis by three strange wanderers. In the pre-revolutionary version of the published epic poems, these strangers reveal themselves as Christ and two apostles. The Soviet version simply removes that revelation.

Interestingly enough, Ilya Muromets was even known in the West. He is found as a legendary hero in some German epic poems of the 13th century. In these poems he is also called Ilya, but he is an exiled *bogatyr* sorrowing after his lost homeland. In the Germanic "Cycle of Ortnit," there is a certain "Ilian von Ruizen" (Ilya the Russian) who takes part in a military campaign and helps Ortnit find a bride. In this story, Ilya has not seen his wife or children for a year, and he speaks of his desire to return to Rus. Another example is the Scandinavian saga written down in Norway c. 1250, called the "Saga of Thidrek", where the bastard son of the ruler of Rus is a man named Ilias, whose half-brother is Valdemar. Thus, according to these literary sources, Ilya Muromets was actually a biological brother of Grand Prince Vladimir of Kiev, the traditional founder of Christianity in Rus.

# 8

# RUSSIAN VALKYRIES: WARRIOR BRIDES OF THE BOGATYRS

**D**espite what you might hear about Russian men being sexist, the folk tradition has tons of strong warrior women. So if you prefer your adventure to follow in the footsteps of one of Russia's fascinating warrior women, this chapter is for you.

## MORE THAN A MATCH FOR THE LEGENDARY BOGATYRS

It wasn't easy for Russian *bogatyrs* to get married. Not every young maid could stand having a hero around. And so, it was often women warriors who captured their hearts. Except, more often than not, these women demanded a wooing equal to the *bogatyrs'* most difficult labors.

Women warriors were such typical characters in Russian folklore that the word "*bogatyrka*" (woman warrior) is even included in the definitive 4-volume dictionary of the Russian language compiled by Vladimir Dal'. The folklorist Afanasiev includes in his collection a story that sounds like Wonder Woman—a garden filled with apples of youth is defended by a nameless band of women warriors. But not all of them were nameless. Here are some of the most famous.

## NASTASYA MIKULISHNA

Dobrynia Nikitich, one of the legendary "three warriors," is famous for his defeat of the giant dragon Zmei Gorynich. But what happened afterward was less glorious for him. He met his future wife, Nastasya Mikulishna, on the way home. She challenged him to a battle and beat him soundly. Not only did she beat him, but she even grabbed him by his golden curls, pulled him off his horse, and stuck him in... her pocket!

Only later did she decide what to do with him. She pulled him out again to see what he looked like. If he was pleasant to look at, she'd marry him. If he was so-so, she'd chop his head off. Lucky for him, he passed the test, and they got married.

In another of the tales, Dobrynia was called to join an embassy to the Golden Horde. Nastasya waited for him to return for twenty years, then received a false report about his death. Prince Vladimir forced her to get married again, this time to Alyosha Popovich, the youngest of the three warriors. She reluctantly agreed. But during the wedding, Dobrynia returned, dressed as a jester, and she recognized him and ran into his embrace.

## VASILISSA MIKULISHNA

Nastasya's siter Vasilissa was no less impressive. She was married to a boyar of Chernigov named Stavr. In a scene reminiscent of *The Taming of the Shrew*, during a feast, Stavr started to boast about his wife's many talents. The problem was that he unfavorably compared Prince Vladimir and his warriors to his much more impressive wife. The prince got angry and imprisoned him.

Finding out about this, Vasilissa came up with a cunning plan. She pretended to be a Tatar youth, brought her warriors with her to Kiev, then demanded the payment of tribute and a princess as her bride. The last was a barb directed at Vladimir, for whom it would be shameful to give a Christian princess to a heathen.

The princess in question suspected that the youth was no youth at all, and she expressed her doubts to Vladimir. So the prince arranged a test of strength, wit, and bravery. Of course, Vasilissa beat everyone, forcing Vladimir to go through with the marriage. But during the pre-wedding feast, the Tatar "youth" sat gloomy at the table. Remembering that the boyar Stavr was an excellent musician, Vladimir called him to perform. At that point, he recognized his wife. Vladimir was forced to admit that all Stavr's boasting about his wife was nothing short of the truth.

## NASTASYA KOROLEVISHNA

The story of Nastasya Korolevishna, the wife of Dunai Ivanovich, is especially dramatic. Dunai traveled to Lithuania with Dobrynia Nikitich to arrange a marriage between Apraksa, daughter of the Lithuanian king, and Prince Vladimir. Dunai, a hothead, said something rude to the king during their time there, and the king imprisoned him. But Dobrynia gathered an army and threatened the kingdom, at which point the king was forced to give him both Apraksa and Dunai.

Apraksa had an older sister, Nastasya. A while before, Dunai had wooed her and nearly paid for it with his life, but she bought the executioners off, giving him time to run away. However, when he returned to take Apraksa back to Kiev, he paid absolutely no attention to Nastasya. She was so mad, she decided to make him pay.

Finding him on the way back to Kiev, she challenged him to single combat, dressed as a foreign knight. Dunai defeated her soundly and was just about to finish her off with a knife when he recognized her. He was so impressed, that he took her back with him to Kiev, where they got married.

THE FAIRY TALES

The most famous woman warrior in Russian fairy tales is Marya Morevna, whom Ivan the Prince wooed after being impressed with her military prowess. Interestingly, though she was probably the better warrior, he still had to rescue her from Koschei the Deathless. Still, this had less to do with his fighting ability, and more with the fact that he needed to atone for his mistakes.

Many historians think that the image of the warrior woman in Russian tales has to do with the early battles between Rus and the Polovetsians. All Polovetsian maidens had to be good with the sword, and their wedding rites included single combat between the groom and the bride. Russian princes often took Polovetsian maidens as their brides, first getting married in the Polovetsian style, then baptizing their brides and getting married the Russian way.

## ❧ 9 ❧

# THE IDIOTIC BRILLIANCE OF
# IVAN THE THIRD SON

You might think we've covered all the possible heroes and heroines in Russian fairy tales. But you'd be wrong. If you really want to succeed in your adventures, I highly recommend that you choose a different kind of hero. A warrior, you ask? A princess who's better at sword fighting than the prince?

Nope. The quintessential hero of Russian fairy tales is Ivan the Idiot.

He's a fool. He's a lazybones. He's filthy. So why is Ivan the Idiot always the winner in the end of the fairy tale? Why does everyone help him get what he needs? Why does the beautiful princess fall in love with him?

FOR THE SAKE OF LAUGHTER

We find the trope of the foolish, yet lucky, youngest brother everywhere. In the spoken tales of European peoples, in Chinese folklore, in the tales of Native Americans, even in African stories. But he gained especial popularity in Russia. Ivan the

Idiot is almost the most prevalent hero of Russian fairy tales. Though this may seem strange, there are plenty of reasons for this.

First of all, he's funny. And oftentimes traveling storytellers of the Middle Ages were also jesters, capable in the arts of the silly. Ivan the Idiot's stories are bizarre. Buckets walk off on their own. A stove traipses about town and tramples people in the streets. A stick rises of its own accord to beat the Tsar's emissaries on the head. It's all ridiculous and grotesque.

At the same time, this is very much typical for the "jester culture" of the time, and not only in Russia. In some ways, Ivan the Idiot is himself a jester.

## THE OPPRESSED IDIOT

The social aspect of the idiot is no less important. After all, he's the youngest son in a patriarchal family. He basically has no rights, no property—nothing of his own. He's on the bottom rung of society. Therefore, the peasants who gathered to listen to the jester-storytellers loved to hear how the oppressed hero, a man with no money, "took it to the Man," so to speak. He not only manages to outwit his older brothers, but ends up defeating important civil servants, princes, and even the Tsar himself!

## IS THE IDIOT A FOOL FOR CHRIST?

Another reason Ivan is so beloved is his similarity to the archetypal fool for Christ. Ivan is an idiot in the old sense of the word, that is, he's crazy. However, he shares many characteristics of the apparently crazy fools for Christ, who assumed the persona of a crazy person as an odd kind of ascetic labor.

At its core, the fool for Christ is "anti-aesthetic," tending toward the ugly. Interestingly, the Russian word "*yurodivy*" (fool for Christ) is related to the word "*urod*," which means "ugly person." Ivan the Idiot is also described as fantastically ugly. He lies on the ledge of the stove all day. He's filthy and his clothes are in tatters. He's constantly wiping snot across his face.

Another similarity between the two is the strangeness of their way of speaking. Here's a typical example from one of the tales:

"Well, a horse has four legs. So does a table. That means that the table will obviously follow me on its own legs."

Other than the comic element, there's something deeper in these kinds of phrases. Ivan turns things on their heads, just as the fools for Christ did. They spoke in riddles or sometimes just babbled nonsense, but always for a purpose. By doing this, they effectively "purified" eternal truths from the chaff of ritualism and familiarity. It's like they're beating a dusty rug to make the colors bright and clean again.

The laziness of Ivan is also interesting. His brothers, who are constantly busy, manage to practically achieve nothing. Ivan, on the other hand, seems to be doing nothing. He sits on the stove and basically reaps the fruits of the labors of his magical helpers. However, the stories don't glorify laziness, rather something more subtle than that.

If the brothers are guided by their reason, Ivan is a creature of impulse, of the heart. He goes "wherever his eyes look, wherever his feet take him." The practical is here opposed to the intuitive. And the latter wins. After all, Ivan doesn't trust in his own useless wits, but only in the will of the divine.

## THE IDIOT AS PAGAN PRIEST

The connection of Ivan the Idiot with the other world is clear. After all, he lies on the ledge of the stove, which is Baba Yaga's favorite resting place. And Baba Yaga is the keeper of the gates of the land of the dead. It's no wonder that magical animals help Ivan, since many of them were totemic beasts in Rus's pagan past. And it's not a surprise that he's the only speaking character who ultimately makes any sense, despite his apparent idiocy.

So if in the more recent past, Ivan's connection with the fool for Christ is clear, in the pagan past, he's most similar to the sorcerer-priest. He's an intermediary between the divine world and the real world, the only one who can speak both languages. He, ironically, is the only one who knows the actual truth. The idiot is the only one who can speak truth when the world has gone mad.

## ❧ 10 ❧

# THE STRANGE AND WONDERFUL
# FOLK TALE OF ST. THEODORE
# THE TYRO

**A**s you navigate the seven obstacles and encounter various mythical creatures, you may sometimes be put in an awkward position. There might be some kind of cat or bird-woman hybrid or something else that will block your way until you... tell them an entertaining story.

And don't think you can get by with the standards. If you're not entertaining, you'll get eaten. Angry witches in particular like to turn people into goats for some reason. (Hey, I didn't write the stories, I just tell them!)

The secret to a good story is to find your inner child. No, really.

Children are the best storytellers. Uninhibited by any rules, they freely mash up everything they know into amazing works of cross-genre brilliance. It's completely normal for my son, for example, to be holding an icon of his saint while telling me a story about the fly who went to the market to buy a samovar, interspersed with a deacon's exclamations from the liturgy, capped with a triumphant bishops' blessing.

Folk tales have the same kind of "child-like" approach to facts—both historical and religious. This is especially obvious in the strange and fascinating folk tale of St. Theodore the

Tyro. That's a great tale to tell to a dangerous mythical creature.

St. Theodore is a saint not particularly remarkable for his life. He is a typical early church martyr. More interesting is the fact that he appeared in a dream to a heretic bishop in the fourth century, managing to prevent entire swathes of the Christian population from eating food defiled by blood from pagan sacrifices (it was Emperor Julian's idea of a sick joke). This event is remembered on the first Friday of every Lent.

But there's also a folk version of St. Theodore the Tyro. The obscure early Roman martyr becomes a full-fledged folk *bogatyr* in a series of six folks songs from different regions of Russia.

Three vivid characters appear in this fanciful version of a history that never was. King Constantin Saúlovich (probably somehow connected with King David), Theodore Tirinin (the king's "favorite child"), and his mother "Theodorisa and Mikitishna."

Here's a combined version of all six tales, taken from Apollon Korinfskii's book *Folk Russia*.

## THE TALE OF ST THEODORE THE TYRO

King Konstantin Saúlovich prayed at the holy Easter service. Suddenly a flaming arrow landed before him. A note hung from it. It told of an enemy force that stood at the gates and threatened to take the holy city of Jerusalem either by surrender or by force.

After the king read these terrifying words, he did not grow afraid in the least. Instead, he came out to the parapet and called out with a great voice:

"You, my great people, all you, my honored guests! Who will stand up for the city of Jerusalem and the true faith, for the mother of God, the Theotokos?"

But not a single warrior answered. The greater hid behind the lesser, and the lesser were long gone. The only one who was brave enough to answer the king's call was a boy.

Then came out his favorite son, the young boy Theodore Tirinin, only twelve years old. To the shame of all the great people, he said to his father, "My dear father, King Constantin Saúlovich! Give me your blessing, give me a brave horse, give me a steel harness, and I will go myself against the host of the enemy!"

The amazed king answered, "Oh, my favorite son, my little man Theodore Tirinin! You have never fought in war, you have never sat on a warhorse, you've never been wounded in body. What is your hope in this dangerous trial?"

"Oh, my beloved father, King Constantin Saúlovich! My hope is in the power of Heaven, and in the mother of God, the Theotokos!"

His father, inspired by his son's bravery, called the boyars to bring him a horse that had never been ridden, the best steel harness, a long spear, and the book of the Gospels. The boy-warrior took these gifts and rode to battle.

For three days and three nights he did not come down from his horse, eating no bread and drinking no water. He defeated the enemy. He vanquished the force of the foe.

But the blood of the enemy rose higher and higher, reaching to his horse's mane, and up to the young warrior's silk belt.

He hurled his spear to the ground, opened the book of the Gospels, but he could not utter a word for his tears, he could not speak aloud for his groaning. But a word finally flew out of his mouth. "Open up, Mother-Earth, from all four sides! Drink the blood of the enemy, do not let us drown in the blood of the foe."

And a miracle occurred, the earth opened under his feet and drank the blood of the enemy.

And the young warrior rode back to the court of his father. His father saw him from the tower of white stone.

"There rides my child, there goes my son! He cannot be

drunk, and yet he rocks back and forth on the back of his horse, and his horse trips as it rides. Or is he shot through to his death?"

Then Theodore rode to his waiting father, and his father took him by the hands and sat him at the king's feast to eat and rest. His mother, feeling sorry for the horse, took it to the wide, blue sea, to wash it of all the blood of the foe. But all of a sudden, a fiery serpent with twelve wings and twelve trunks ate the brave horse and carried away Theodore's mother to its caves, as a wet-nurse to its twelve baby serpents.

Two angels of God appeared and spoke in human voices to Theodore. "O you, young warrior Theodore Tirinin. You sit here, feasting, and you do not know the calamity that has befallen. A serpent of fire has taken your mother, eaten your horse!"

The news struck the child-warrior like thunder in the middle of a clear day. The food turned to ashes in his mouth. He took his harness and his weapons, and he rode far away into the mountains. He rode to the shores of the blue sea, and there was no way forward for the young warrior.

But he did not lose heart. Once again he thrust his spear into the earth and opened the book of the Gospels. Listening to his holy prayers, a great fish, a whale came up from the depths and spoke with a human voice.

"O man, Theodore Tirinin, walk on my back as on dry land!"

The young man listened to the words of the whale and walked on its back, leaning on its spear. He approached the caves of the serpent, where his mother was wet-nurse to the twelve baby serpents. He struck and killed the twelve baby serpents and took his mother and carried her over the blue sea, walking on the whale's back as on dry land.

But it was not yet time for Theodore to rest from his labors. The serpent of fire flew overhead, filling the warrior's mother's heart with dread.

"Oh my sweet child," she exclaimed, "we have perished. Here comes the serpent of fire, with twelve terrible wings and trunks!"

But Theodore Tirinin did not fear the serpent. He nocked an arrow to his bow, fired it at the flying beast, and he pierced through its heart and liver. And again the blood came flowing down, threatening to drown them. And once again Theodore prayed, and Mother-Earth opened up and drank the enemy's blood dry.

Theodore and his mother arrived at the gates of Jerusalem. King Constantin Saúlovich ordered the bells to be rung in all the churches, services of thanksgiving to be served in all the temples.

But Theodore Tirinin, mindful of the time of year, rebuked his father.

"O, my dear father, King Constantin Saúlovich! Do not ring the bells in the churches, do not serve the services of thanksgiving. Remember, Orthodox people, that it's the first week of Lent! Whoever fittingly celebrates this first week of Lent, the Lord Himself will write his name in the book of life. He will be freed from the torments of hell, and he will inherit the kingdom of heaven!"

The triumphant end of the song-story is this:

"Let us sing the praise of Theodore. His praise will never fade for all ages. And unto the ages of ages! Have mercy on us!"

# HOW TO BECOME AN EPIC
# STORYTELLER

S o you managed to get past the monster by telling the story of St. Theodore.

But what if you got a particularly cantankerous mythical creature, who wants more than one tale? Well, it might be a good idea to become an epic Russian storyteller in your own right. Here's what you have to do.

❧

## BE BORN IN THE RIGHT PLACE

First of all, dear future storyteller, you have to listen to as many existing *bylini* (epic Russian poems) in as many different version as you can. Since it's an orally-transmitted form of art, you have no choice but to memorize the expansive list of heroes and villains and story tropes (which is why you're reading this book in the first place, right?).

In the Russian North, *bylini* were often told (i.e. sung) during times of common work—fishing in bulk for the winter or hunting, for example. If you're especially lucky, you will have been born in the 19th century not far from Lake Ona. Or you live, perhaps, on the banks of the White Sea. When it's bad weather, no one goes outside in the Russian North. Perfect time for the fishermen and hunters to hear all the labors and adventures of the Russian *bogatyrs*. Interestingly, even in the second half of the 20th century, when the art of epic poetry had died out, fishermen still took a librarian with them out to the long-term fishing season.

❦

## BE BORN IN A DYNASTY OF STORYTELLERS

Epic poetry was sometimes performed as entertainment for children. In the memoirs of the professional storyteller Maria Dmitrievna Krivopolenova, she describes this scene:

"The kids annoyed grandfather in the evening, asking him to sing of the old days. At first, grandfather sang a short one, but then he sang one of the long ones."

❦

## ORIENT YOURSELF IN THE EPIC WORLD

Without understanding the reality of the world of epic poetry—who rode where, who battled whom—you will never become a good storyteller. You will mix up names, places, and you will never be accepted by the extremely choosy zealots of the tradition (or, as we already mentioned, you might get eaten). You have to know that even geography is specifically connected to character. For example, Prince Vladimir is in Kiev, while Sadko is in Novgorod.

You also have to understand the movements of common epic journeys. For example, Vasili Buslaevich travels to Jerusalem, while Ilya Muromets always rides from Murom, through Chernigov, into Kiev.

The names in the *bylini* are strictly determined by this dichotomy—"one of ours" (good) vs. "one of theirs" (very bad). In other words, every hero has his own very specific antagonist. Ilya Muromets, for example, can never battle Tugarin Zmei (that's Alyosha Popovich's job). Neither can Dobrynia Nikitich battle the dog Kalin-Tsar. You must never allow such mistakes. People don't like a bad storyteller. There have even been cases when a bad storyteller was literally beaten out of a village.

## LEARN TO IMPROVISE

Albert Lord, a folklorist who studied the epic traditions of the South Slavs, determined that there are three stages of studying to be a storyteller:

1. 1.Passive listening
2. 2.Active repetition
3. 3.Intentional improvisation

How can a storyteller learn hundreds upon hundreds of lines of text? Why are there different versions of the same *bylina*? What elements needed to be kept the same, but what could be changed?

It's important to understand that an epic poem doesn't exist in a kind of ossified "final form." Every performance was literally a new creation. Folklorists have determined that the tropes of epic poetry and the specific lexicon that is used to create the poems are not memorized. Rather, they are constructed anew every time, just as phrases in everyday conversation are. This means that the storyteller invents a story in the process of singing. It's like he's weaving pearls into a tapestry.

So. How do you do this? Find the best storytellers in your area. Begin by copying their mannerisms and repertoire. Later, once you've become familiar with it all, you can begin to improvise. But make sure your improvisation is fully within the existing geography and episodic structure. Don't invent. Improvise.

## SOMETIMES YOUR ARE ALLOWED TO READ

If you can only find one or two professional storytellers in your area, and you still want to become a real storyteller, you'll have to read. There are many good collections of epic poetry out there. They first became popular in the 19th century, when cheap editions were printed by the thousands. Then, many so-called storytellers tried to pass themselves off as professionals in folkloric circles. In actual fact, all they did was memorize the poems from the popular editions.

One positive aspect of this was that epic poetry was once again performed as it should be—sung aloud. And many real storytellers found this to be a gold mine of new possible interpretations of characters and events. Yuri Novikov, a folklorist, found more than 320 new versions of sung epic poems that had elements borrowed from the printed editions.

## OTHERWISE...

If you can't follow all of the steps above, you're out of luck for Russian epic poetry. It never found any other method of transmission. However, you can still learn other traditions. For example, European epic poets, Yakut Olonkho singers, the Kazakh *akyn*, and the Khakaz *khaidja* all receive their gift either in their sleep (like the Anglo-Saxon poet Caedmon), or after meeting a man in white robes (as the Khakaz *khaidja* Stepan Yegorovich Burnakov), or by drinking the water in a sacred well (as the Uzbek *bakshas*). So, as long as you're not Russian, you can always hope for a divine gift...

# 12

# THE LAND OF THE DEAD

B ut what about our destination? What is the magical kingdom at the end of our journey? Well, don't be too upset. Unfortunately, it's the land of the dead.

## FIRE AND WATER

Ancient Russians imagined the passage between life and death as either crossing a river or going through fire. The Slavic word for "heaven" (*rai*) is actually pre-Christian. The words for heaven and "river" are etymologically connected. Originally, *rai* is the place beyond flowing water, the place where birds flew during winter.

Ancient Slavs also imagined heaven as a beautiful garden filled with apple trees. The apples were always golden, giving eternal youth, health, and beauty. It can also be the country beyond the sea (the sea being a very distant place in Steppe-bound Russia), or the country at the rising of the sun. Many-headed serpents guard access to the country of eternal summer, the source of living water. This is exactly where all the heroes must go to achieve their goal.

## THE KEEPERS OF HEAVEN'S KEYS

Pre-Christian Slavs believed that their righteous ancestors lived in the sky. The keys to this heavenly realm were kept by birds who locked "heaven" when they left for winter. When they came back in spring, they opened the doors, and the sources of living water came flowing down as rain. This rain then brought the earth back to life with the coming spring.

No living man can cross into the world of the dead. Only mythical heroes can overcome the border. Later, the heroes of fairy tales also had the chance, though not all of them made it.

## ONE-EYED FATE

If Baba Yaga is an ambivalent character that can either help you get to the land of the dead or cook you and make soup out of you, Fate is unequivocally evil. In the Russian tales, Fate comes in the form of Likho the one-eyed, who is sometimes depicted as a giant old woman. She eats people and sleeps on a bed of bones. If Likho stands up, her head reaches higher than the trees. But she can also take the form of a normal woman, except with one eye. The hero that meets her often loses an arm or a leg, and sometimes his life. So watch out.

But Likho is not death, she only serves death. We see this in an ancient pagan Russian rite. During epidemics, villagers would build a sacrificial fire kindled from a vaguely feminine idol with a single eye. So it wasn't "death" that they burned, but death's servant. Only later was Likho explicitly connected with "evil fate."

## CROSSING INTO THE LAND OF THE DEAD

When you meet Baba Yaga, you have to go through a kind of rite of initiation. Initially, Baba Yaga asks three riddles, and the wrong answer means death. The riddling game can also be three trials or menial tasks. Only after their completion does she become helpful.

Baba Yaga's hut sits on the border between the lands of the living and the dead. The fact that it faces away from the hero (you actually have to talk to it to get it to turn around) shows that it belongs more to the land of the dead than the living. Only the magic words can get it to turn around.

There are ancient historical models for the "hut on chicken feet". In each village, there was a house built on a raised platform where various rites of passage were conducted for children entering adulthood. They were sacred houses, only to be entered by the consecrated. Whoever entered them, "died" to their previous life and came back "resurrected" as adults.

⚜

## THE LAND OF THE DEAD

The Slavic land of the dead shares some features with the Hades of Greek Mythology. It has nothing in common with the Christian hell. It's found inside the earth, and it is not the place of evil spirits. Evil spirits are found under the earth itself, and they can harm both those who live in the earth (the dead) and those who live above it (the living).

Thus, the land of the dead has two levels—the level of ancestors and the level of the evil powers. However, heroes can also find the world of the dead at the edge of the world and in the sky.

As for the lord of that scary place... Well, buckle up. It's time to meet Koschei the Deathless.

# 13

# THE LORD OF DEATH'S
# KINGDOM

Koschei the Deathless. He's the quintessential fairy tale villain. He is death itself, as well as being the lord of the kingdom of the dead. And if you want to get to the end of your story, you'll need to get to it over his dead body.

His name is taken from a Turkic word meaning "slave." The word "koshchi" occurs in Russian chronicles as early as the 12th century, where it means "servant." In the famous epic poem *The Lay of Prince Igor*, the word more specifically means a prisoner of war:

"Igor the prince dismounted from his golden saddle and sat in the slave's saddle." (In other words, Prince Igor was captured in war)

Koshchei the Deathless is a demonic figure. He is an incarnation of black magic, evil cunning, and ingratitude. He is also like a dragon in the sense that he hoards treasure, but never uses it for himself. Also like a dragon, he has the habit of stealing princesses and marrying them.

We see Koschei's connection with the world of the dead in various fairy tales. In "Maria Morevna," he is the prisoner of the eponymous warrior-princess. Her own name is synonymous with death. "Mara" is an ancient death-bearing mythical creature, and "mor" is another word for "fatal plague."

Maria forbids her husband, Ivan the Prince, from entering the room where Koshchei is bound. Naturally, the foolish Ivan can't contain himself and goes snooping. He sees Koshchei tied up with twelve chains (this story is retold by a hag in my first novel). Taking pity on the skeletal old man, he unwittingly frees him. Koshchei thanks him by stealing his wife and taking her off to the land of the dead.

Interestingly, Ivan's helper in this tale is none other than Baba Yaga. She first must test him (as you already know). But after he passes the ordeal, Baba Yaga gives him a magic horse. Other helpers along the way include an eagle (a symbol for wind), a falcon (a symbol for thunder), and a crow (rain or hail). Twice Ivan fails to return with his wife. Only the third time does the magic horse kill Koshchei with its hoof.

The kidnapping of Maria Morevna, in a mythological sense, has to do with the cycles of winter and spring. In one of the versions of this tale, Ivan can't find Maria the first two times he searches for her. Some ethnographers believe this refers to the period in summer and fall when farmers sow and harvest their crops. As Ivan's horse says:

"You can plant your wheat, wait for it to grow, harvest it, grind it, turn it into flour, bake five breads, eat those breads, and then go catch her. You'll still have more than enough time!"

Koshchei is often burned at the end of the tales, and his ashes are spread over the fields. This is another connection with the world of the dead. Casting the ashes of a burnt effigy of winter over a spring field is an ancient Slavic ritual to encourage good harvests.

Another interesting object that's often associated with the rebirth of spring is the egg, which was believed to have magical powers. Like a seed that's thrown into the ground, an egg has to "die" before it can give "new life." According to the Slavs' dualistic worldview, the world in general, like the egg in particular, contain the principles of life and death equally. To this day, people leave eggs at cemeteries.

The hiding of Koshchei's death inside the egg (a common fairy tale trope) reflects this dualistic worldview, in which the powers of light and the powers of dark are always in conflict. Life and death go through cycles of victory and defeat. Death can never be destroyed fully. Even though Koshchei always dies, he always comes back in the next tale. However, that doesn't mean you shouldn't fight death. The battle with evil releases the power of life and confirms it.

This eternal conflict between good and evil is also reflected in the descriptions of Koshchei's kingdom of death. It's often at the edge of the world, in a castle with golden windows and crystal doors. In the castle, there are many precious stones. A slave serves Koshchei. A dark army stands ready at his call. As you see, there are both "light" and "dark" aspects to this description of Koshchei's land.

In the oldest tales, Koshchei's antagonist is named "Anastasya" or "Maria". If "Maria" has to do with death, "Anastasya" means "the resurrected one." Interestingly, the hero who helps Anastasya has a special patronymic: Godinych. The word "god," which now means "year," used to mean "time in general." Ivan Godinych, in this sense, marries Anastasya in the end, taking her away from Koshchei's kingdom, thereby "resurrecting" the world for summer's time (like the myth of Persephone and Hades).

In this version of the tale, Ivan and Koshchei have a duel, and Ivan wins. But cunning Koshchei manages to convince Anastasya to help him, and he manages to tie Ivan to an oak. A bird of prophecy then lands on the oak tree, and announces that Koshchei has no power over Anastasya. The irate Koshchei shoots at the bird, but Ivan convinces the arrow to kill Koshchei instead. Angry at Anastasya's betrayal, Ivan actually kills her.

All this brutality has everything to do with the cycles of nature. Nature dies, nature resurrects, and then it dies again.

Death and chaos, the inhabitants of the invisible world, are always trying to invade the visible world. The mythical journey of the hero unites these two worlds. The hero must enter the fray alone against the personified forces of evil and chaos. Naturally, he wins in the end, but his enemies always come back in the next tale.

All this interesting, no doubt. But how do you actually kill Koschei?

⚜

## HOW TO KILL THE DEATHLESS ONE

In one of the tales, Koshchei incautiously reveals:

"My death is far off: on the ocean, on the sea, there is an island, on that island there is an oak, under that oak tree is buried a chest, in that chest is a hare, in that hare – a duck, in that duck – an egg. And in that egg is my death."

The problem is that the oak is too tall to climb, the chest is impossible to break, the hare is faster than you'll ever be, the duck can fly faster than you can run.

I did say it would be hard, didn't I?

The trick is found in many of the tales. You need to be kind to all animals you meet, especially the ones that talk. If you're lucky, you'll find and make friends with the following:

- A bear, who will tear the oak down for you and break the chest open
- A wolf, who will tear the hare in two
- A falcon, who will tear the duck in two
- When the egg falls out of the duck and into the sea, don't cry. Because you've made friends with a pike, who will catch it for you and hand it back to you.

Then, all you need to do is crack open the egg and snap the thin needle inside.

Many academics understand this "nesting doll" structure to represent a vision of the universe. Thus, the seas and oceans represent water, the island is the land, the oak is the plants, the hare is the animals, the duck is the birds. The oak also represents the "tree of the world."

In other words, the only way to kill Koshchei is to destroy the cosmos. This may be why he never really dies, but always comes back to haunt the heroes of the tales.

# ❧ 14 ❧

## RUSSIAN FOLKLORE... OR
## FAKELORE?

S o. You now know how to reach the land of the dead, kill the deathless one, and win riches and renown.

Now for the tricky bit. You might read some stories or encounter some mythical figures that are...well, fake.

Russian fairy tales are *ancient*. Some scholars believe many of them date from a period before the Christianization of Russia (988 AD), being a kind of cultural bridge from paganism to Christianity. You might think that having a rich tradition of epics and fairy tales would be a source of pride for Russians.

But you may know about Russians' famous contrariness? And their tendency toward excessive self-loathing? Yes, it's a thing.

So in the 18th century, Russia entered the grand stage of European history. It threw aside its "primitive Easternness", and did everything possible to become as European as possible. Since Russia had no real Renaissance (like Western Europe), the young empire felt like it lacked something. It lacked a pagan, classical past to be reborn in a Russian renaissance. But Russian paganism and mythology never developed along the path of the Greeks. There was not even a pantheon (not really), nor were there any established myths about the gods. Still, the historians of the time thought it might be possible to reconstruct such a pantheon, and give the Russians their proper classical past.

They gathered all the information they could. But there were more gaps than there were myths. Wherever they would find a gap, they would simply invent things. And so, Russian "armchair mythology" or "fake-lore" was born. It became a kaleidoscope of made-up gods that either never existed or were so twisted into badly-fitting models that they became unrecognizable.

The well-known character from fairy tales, Baba Yaga, became "a goddess of the underworld," who required sacrifices of blood for her "granddaughters". The house spirits (*domovie*) and forest spirits (*leshye*) of popular tales became "demigods." Here's the hodgepodge they came up with:

- Popular divinities of Western Slavs
- The wooden idols of Kievan Rus
- Effigies built (and burnt) during the Carnival period before Lent
- The cryptic character of Boyan from the epic poem "The Lay of Prince Igor"
- pagan priests from fake historical chronicles
- Other completely made-up gods

Effectively, the historians made up a Russian "Olympus." Some of these fake gods continue to exist in the popular imagination to this day. Here are some of the highlights.

## USLAD

Here's how Grigory Glinka, one of the founders of Russian "fake-lore," described this completely made-up god:

"He had a happy face, a red tinge to his cheeks, a wide smile, crowned with flowers, dressed lazily in a tunic, playing a hand-held harp, and dancing to his own music. He is the god of happiness and earthly pleasures."

Sound familiar? Obviously, this is nothing more than a Russian Bacchus. The god of wine and partying.

How did such a non-Russian god appear in the "Russian pantheon?" *The Chronicle of Past Times*, one of the only historical records of early Russian history, tells of the first religious reforms of St. Vladimir of Kiev. He wanted to unify the various forms of paganism of the Russians (it didn't work). The writer of the Chronicle lists the idols that Vladimir "sanctioned" and built on the shores of the Dniepr, the first of which was Perun (the Slavic counterpart to Thor), who was described as having "golden lips" (*ust zlat*).

In the 16th century, one of the early manuscripts of the *Chronicle* made its way into the hands of a certain Austrian baron and writer named Sigizmund von Gerberstein. He didn't speak Russian (he did speak Slovenian), and he didn't quite understand what he was reading. When he came to the description of Perun, he thought that "*ust zlat*" (golden lips) was a separate god in Vladimir's pantheon. Perfect for Russian "fake-lore!" Let's make him a Slavic Bacchus!

## ZIMTSERLA

This fake goddess was first found in another incorrectly rewritten listing of Vladimir's pantheon. One of the idols was "Semargl", which was incorrectly rendered in Romance characters as "Simaergla," then rewritten again mistakenly by a Russian scribe to become "Zimtserla." Someone noticed that the new version of this goddess is made up of the words "winter" and "wipe out" (Zima and stert'). So, obviously, she would make a perfect goddess of spring and flowers.

So she became a Russian version of Persephone, but without the wonderful myth.

## LEL'

In the "fake-lore" of the 18th century, this god was the "demigod of divine ardor." He appears in Pushkin's Ruslan and Ludmilla as a divine patron of the marriage bed. But his most significant appearance is in Ostrovskii's "Snow Maiden," where this golden-haired Slavic Cupid runs rampant throughout the play.

Where did he come from? Most likely, from folk wedding songs. In the refrains, there was a nonsense syllable (common enough in Russian songs) that sounded like this: "lel'-polel', liuli-lel'". This was probably was a folk bastardization of "Halleluia." Polish historians of the 16th century, not understanding that this was nonsense, made up an entire family of gods from these nonsense-refrains. Lel' was the god of love, Polel' was his brother and the patron of marriages, and their mother was Lada. By the 18th century, the creators of Russian "fake-lore" decided that these Polish phantoms were worthy of inclusion into the "Slavic Olympus."

## YARILO

In the already-mentioned play by Ostrovskii, Yarilo is a god of fire, all-knowing and irascible. After the Snow Maiden dies and the order of the world is restored, Yarilo appears to his followers on his holy mountain. He looks like this:

"A young man in white clothing. In his right hand is a shining human head, and in his left is a sheaf of barley."

Actually, Yarilo was a rarely-encountered harvest god

worshiped in certain areas of southern Russia. It's also the name given to the straw effigy of an old woman burned during Carnival. In other regions, she was a symbol of fertility buried or burned to symbolize the end of the time for physical pleasures, and the beginning of Lent.

In these folk traditions of certain regions, the "fake-lorists" thought they saw the signs of a genuine sun god, and they ran with the idea. Ironically, today's Russian neo-pagans, unaware of his dubious origins, do worship him as the god of sun and fire.

## RADEGAST

At the beginning of the 19th century, the origin of the Slavs was hotly debated. Some historians believed in Slavic runes and a legendary city called Petra. What caused this argument was the discovery of bronze figurines in 1768 in the village of Prilwitza in Mecklenburg. Among the figurines was an image of Radegast, a god found in some medieval chronicles. His chest is covered by a shield with a bull's head, and his helmet is crowned by the form of a bird.

Very soon afterward, it turned out that the figurines were a hoax. Moreover, today's folklorists doubt that Radegast was ever a god of the Slavs at all. But he still made it into the pantheon of the fake Russian gods!

All this to say that it's probably best not to fit other cultures' patterns onto your own, especially when your own culture has a lot to offer. The rest of this little booklet is a short glimpse into the world of Russian fairy tales and epics, a world beautiful and strange in its own right.

## 🐾 15 🐾

# THE SPRITUAL MEANING OF
# STORIES

I hope you've enjoyed this somewhat cheeky guide to how to survive Russian fairy tales. But to be serious for a moment, these stories contain much more than meets the eye. Even if they're chaotic, bizarre, and frequently silly, there's a depth to them, simmering under the surface, that points to something quite profound.

This depth is beautifully described by the Russian philosopher and writer Ivan Ilyin in a lecture he gave in the 30's, which he called *The Spiritual Meaning of Stories.*

One more thing. His point about the folklore of a country springing up from the deep history of a nation–this is something very important for all of us Americans to think about, especially since so many of our cultural elites seem to be more interested in putting down or even destroying our common culture (such as it is) rather than returning to it as a well of inspiration. Something to think about.

## THE SPIRITUAL MEANING OF STORIES, A LECTURE BY IVAN ILYIN (TRANSLATED BY NICHOLAS KOTAR)

Whatever shadow may fall on your life—maybe you are worried about the fate of your country, or perhaps dark thoughts visit you concerning your own future, or maybe your entire life seems an unbearable wound—remember the Russian fairy tale. Listen to her quiet, ancient, wise voice.

Don't think the fairy tale is a childish diversion, not worthy of the attention of a grown man. And don't think that adults are smart, and children stupid. Don't imagine that an adult has to "stupefy" himself to tell a story to a child.

Is it not perhaps the opposite? Aren't our minds the source of most of our woes? And what is stupidity, anyway? Is all stupidity dangerous or shameful? Or is there perhaps an intelligent kind of stupidity, something desirable and blessed that begins with stupidity but ends with wisdom? Maybe there are two kinds of stupidity? One comes from blind self-contentment, the other from a healthy skepticism? One stupefies with pride and leads to vulgarity, while the other stupefies through humility and leads to wisdom...

This sort of stupidity, or perhaps better called *simplicity*, exactly describes all folk tales, especially Russian folk tales.

The fairy tale doesn't insist on anything. It doesn't intrude on anyone. It's not in the least contrived. If you don't want to listen, don't! It's like a flower, but not one from a cultivated garden. It's like a wildflower in the field that sows itself, that roots itself, that pushes its own flower petals up toward God's sunlight. This flower gives its own kind of honey, a wondrous and fragrant honey that only a simple and wise beekeeper can harvest.

The same is true of the spiritual meaning of the fairy tale. It's like refined and sweet-smelling honey. If you drip it on your tongue, you'll taste all the ineffable essence of Russia's nature—the smell of the earth, the heat of the sun, the fragrance of flowers, and something else that is subtle and rich, something eternally youthful and yet eternally ancient. All this, in its ineffable taste and smell.

This fragrance has accumulated over hundreds of years inside the souls of people, inside Russian souls that have invisibly flowered and wilted on the plains of that wide land. The Russian fairy tale conceals within itself hundreds and thousands of years of its people's spiritual experience. The history of the Russian people is only one thousand years old; however, the age of a nation isn't limited by the memory of its history. After all, one thousand years ago, Russia only awoke to itself and began to think of itself as a nation, and only after it was baptized.

Russia retained little memory of its pre-Christian past. But this past, lost to its memory, wasn't lost to the Russian spirit. Everything that happened before, lost to the memory, the Russian people took with them and carried into their history. This is not the Chronicle or the epic poem, not the life of a saint or a legend. This is the fairy tale.

No, none of it every actually happened. Never and nowhere did these princes and warriors live. None of these grey wolves or deathless spirits ever existed. None of these Baba Yagas or Zmei Goryniches or Ivan the Fools ever walked the Russian land. And only he who studies the science of history but cuts ties with the science of spiritual experience thinks fairy tales are stupid.

Only he who worships at the altar of facts and has lost the ability to contemplate a state of being ignores fairy tales. Only the one who wants to see with his physical eyes alone, plucking out his spiritual eyes in the process, considers the fairy tale to be dead.

Fine. Let's call the fairy tale simplistic. But it is at least modest in its simplicity. And for its modesty, we forgive it its stupidity. After all, it takes courage to be so simple! The fairy tale doesn't hide its inaccuracies. It isn't ashamed of its simplicity. It's not afraid of strict questions and mocking smiles.

Finally, we forgive fairy tales because they believe in their own way of seeing the world. The fairy tale considers the events of its own telling with reverence. It lives by its images and awaits its resolution, its final sigh, in the sincerity of those same images.

Fairy tales are sincere, and so we forgive them. Like sparks that fly from a bonfire and light up the darkness, so also the vision of stories flies up directly from the hearts of the people, from their loves and hatreds, from their fears and hopes. Having flown up from those depths, stories illuminate the grayness and darkness of everyday life.

The themes of these stories reside in the wise depths of human instinct, somewhere deep inside those holy depths, where the knots of national essence and national character reside, and where they await their final resolution, completion, and freedom. No proud man, no coward, no faithless, crooked soul can plumb these depths of national-spiritual experience. Only the trusting, sincere, contemplative simpleton, brave in his poetic seriousness, can reach those depths and come out from there rich with fairy tales.

For such a man, these fairy tales are not fabrications or tall tales, but poetic illumination, essential reality, even the beginning of all philosophy. Fairy tales don't become obsolete if we lose the wisdom to live by it. No, it is we who have perverted our emotional and spiritual culture. And *we* will dissipate and die off if we lose our access to these tales.

What is this access to fairy tales? What must we do to make the fairy tale, like the house on chicken feet, "turn its back to the forest and face us?" How can we see it and live by it, how can we illuminate its oracular depth and make clear its true spiritual meaning?

For this, we must not cling to the sober mind of the daylight consciousness with all its observations, its generalizations, its "laws of nature." The fairy tale sees the world in a different way. It sees other ways of being.

It sees *less*, because it only sees short, simplified, concentrated fragments from the lives of heroes. This brevity is the result of a creative reduction. The story can be told in twenty minutes, but it encompasses twenty years, perhaps. After all, as the storytellers said, "quickly is the story told, but slowly does the story unfold." The fairy tale's brevity is artistic. Its simplicity is stylized. Its concentration is symbolic. For the fairy tale is a fragment of national art.

The story itself is already art. It conceals and reveals in its words an entire world of images, and these images symbolize profound spiritual states. But at the same time, the fairy tale is not quite art, because it is alive, for it is passed from teller to teller, and has no single, complete, concrete version. Anyone has the right to tell the fairy tale in his own way, as he sees fit. Therefore, the fairy tale is a kind of national theme for *personal dreaming*.

This makes the fairy tale like myths, and like songs, and like decorations on embroidery or on the roofs of those fanciful Russian houses. The myth says to the poet, "Take me into your contemplation and give me a final form and body." And Homer, Ovid, Goethe, Wagner, and Pushkin all answered the myth. The song says to all singers, "Take me with your hearing and your soul and sing me from your own depths, as God inspires you." And all minstrels, minnesingers, harpists, and folk composers answer the call.

The ornament says to the master artisan, "Here I am! Describe your way of life through my design." And all folk artists, woodworkers, ironworkers, from Siena to Archangelsk, answer the call.

This is the psychological place of the fairy tale. It is a kind of art similar to myths, songs, and ornamentation. It comes from the same place as dreams, premonitions, and prophecies. This is why the birth of a story is at the same time artistic and magical. It not only tells a story, but it sings it into being. And the more a fairy tale sings, the easier it enters the soul, and the stronger is its magical force to calm, order, and illumine the soul. The fairy tale comes from the same source as the songs of mages, with their commanding power. This is why stories repeat phrases and images so often.

This is also why the greatest Russian poets, Zhukovskii and Pushkin, sang their favorite stories in verse, imbuing the national myth with the force of magical song and telling the fairy tale in the perfect ornamentation of their own words.

But the fairy tale sees a great deal *more* also than the daylight consciousness. Nature and its daylight consciousness have their own essential inevitability and their own natural impossibilities. But the fairy tale is limited neither by inevitability nor by impossibility. It has its *own*"inevitabilities" and "impossibilities." These are different, spiritual, internal, mysterious.

The fairy tale doesn't submit to the laws of nature or gravity or time or space. It only submits to the laws of creative imagination and the laws of the national-heroic epic. It submits to the laws of magic. It is laid down by the laws of prophetic dreaming, inspired ecstasy, and illumination from contemplation. These laws are mystical. You can sense them, but you can't easily formulate them. Their power, however, is eternal and world-creating. These are the things that make a fairy tale live and breathe.

So, don't listen to a fairy tale in the bright light of day or with your prosaic and wing-less consciousness. Listen to a fairy tale in the evening or at night, in the magical darkness that removes familiarity from things and gives them a new, unexpected, mysterious form. You should listen to fairy tales with the dusky consciousness between sleeping and waking. Listen from the depth of your unconscious mind, where your soul lives like a child, where it's childishly "stupid" and isn't ashamed of its stupidity, where it enters into the story with complete seriousness and a passion of hope and despair, not even remembering that it's all make believe.

There, you'll find life itself- the battle, the victory, and *the end*.

## Coming soon...

A new podcast featuring Nicholas Kotar reading classic Slavic fairy tales retold for a modern audience. To be the first to hear about launch date, join Nicholas Kotar's Readers' Group. You'll also receive a FREE novella in the universe of Kotar's *Raven Son* epic fantasy series. Just visit nicholaskotar.com for more information.

ALSO BY NICHOLAS KOTAR

*The Song of the Sirin*
*The Curse of the Raven*
*The Heart of the World*
*The Forge of the Covenant*

# ABOUT THE AUTHOR

Nicholas Kotar is a writer of epic fantasy inspired by Russian fairy tales, a freelance translator from Russian to English, the resident conductor of the men's choir at a Russian monastery in the middle of nowhere, and a semi-professional vocalist. His one great regret in life is that he was not born in the nineteenth century in St. Petersburg, but he is doing everything he can to remedy that error.

Made in the USA
Coppell, TX
17 December 2020